WRITTEN AND ILLUSTRATED BY

PETER PAUPER PRESS
Fine Books and Gifts Since 1928

OUR COMPANY

IN 1928, AT THE AGE OF TWENTY-TWO, PETER BEILENSON BEGAN PRINTING BOOKS ON A SMALL PRESS IN THE BASEMENT OF HIS PARENTS' HOME IN LARCHMONT, NEW YORK. PETER—AND LATER, HIS WIFE, EDNA—SOUGHT TO CREATE FINE BOOKS THAT SOLD AT "PRICES EVEN A PAUPER COULD AFFORD."

TODAY, STILL FAMILY OWNED AND OPERATED, PETER PAUPER PRESS CONTINUES TO HONOR OUR FOUNDERS' LEGACY AND OUR CUSTOMERS' EXPECTATIONS OF BEAUTY, QUALITY, AND VALUE.

o o o

DESIGNED BY DAVID COLE WHEELER

COPYRIGHT © 2020
PETER PAUPER PRESS, INC.
202 MAMARONECK AVENUE
WHITE PLAINS, NY 10601 USA
ALL RIGHTS RESERVED
ISBN 978-1-4413-3292-9
PRINTED IN CHINA
7

VISIT US AT WWW.PETERPAUPER.COM

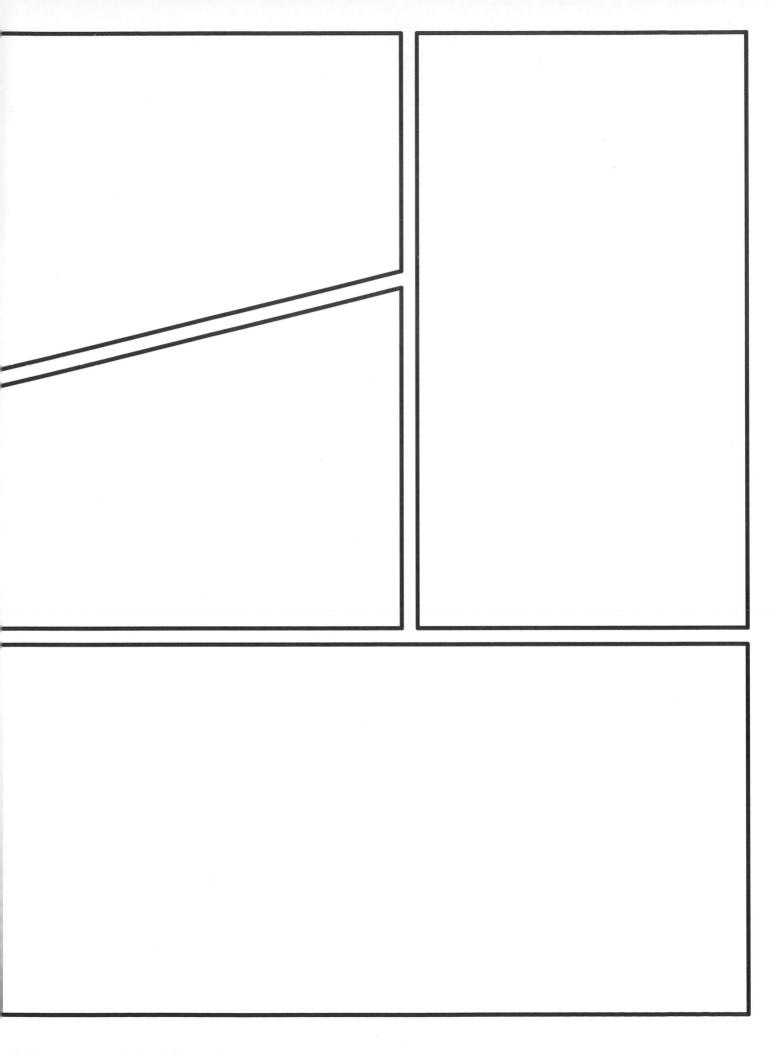

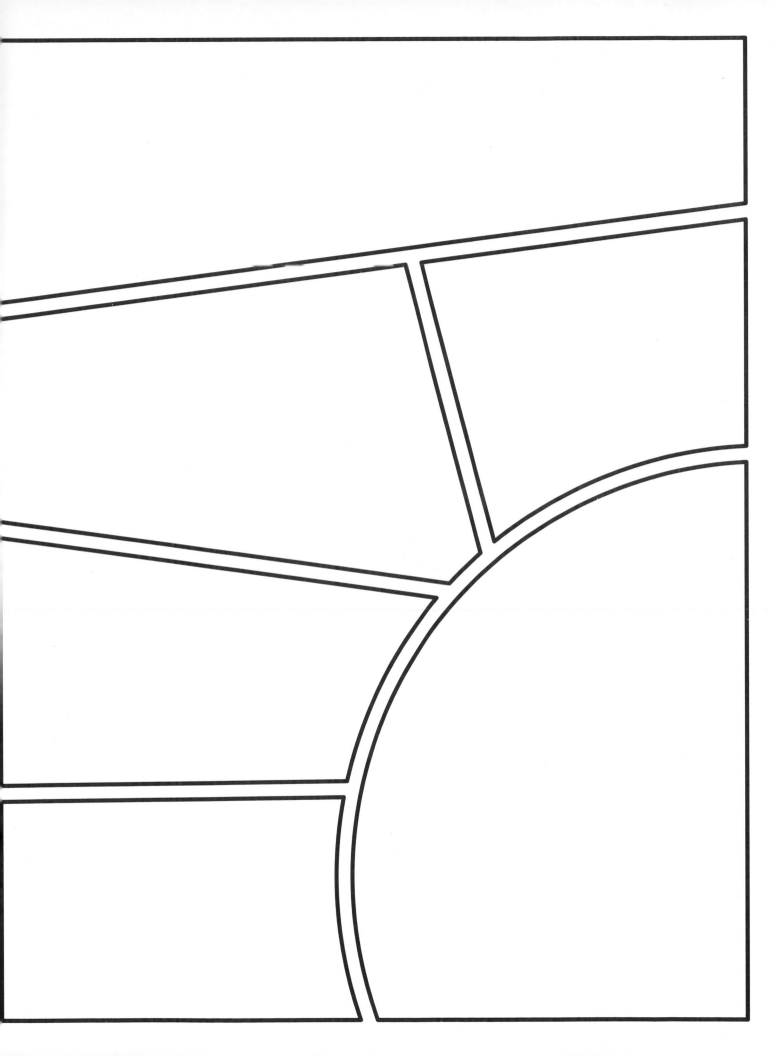

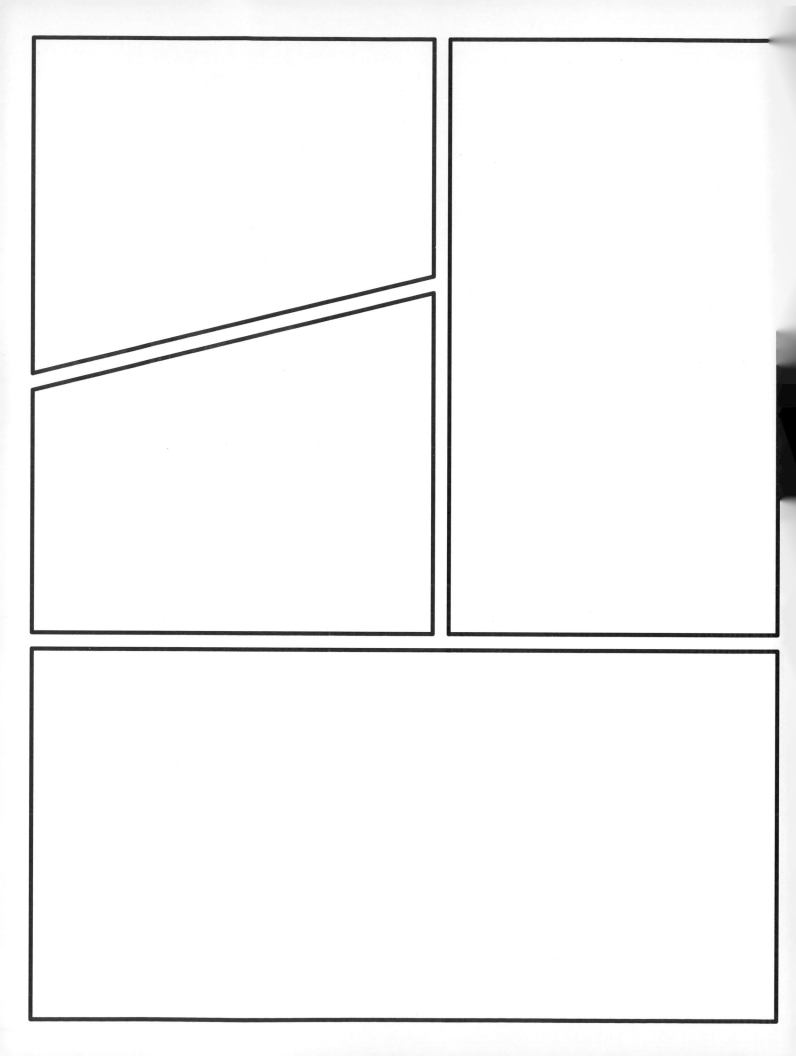

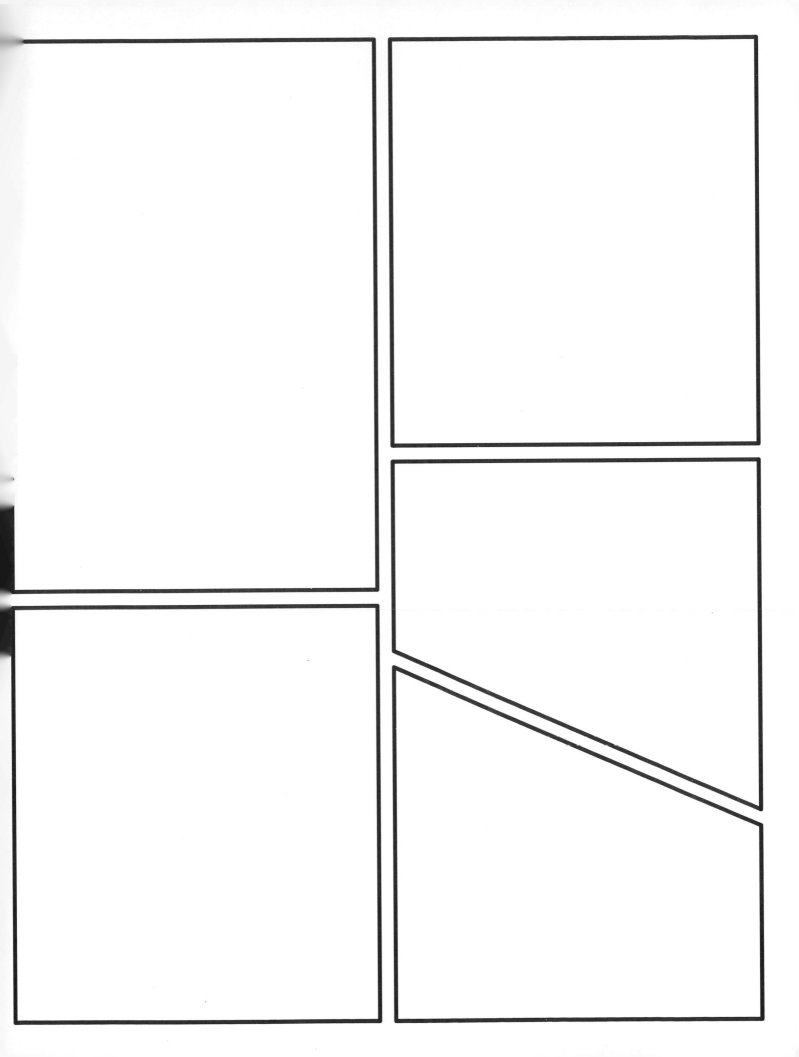

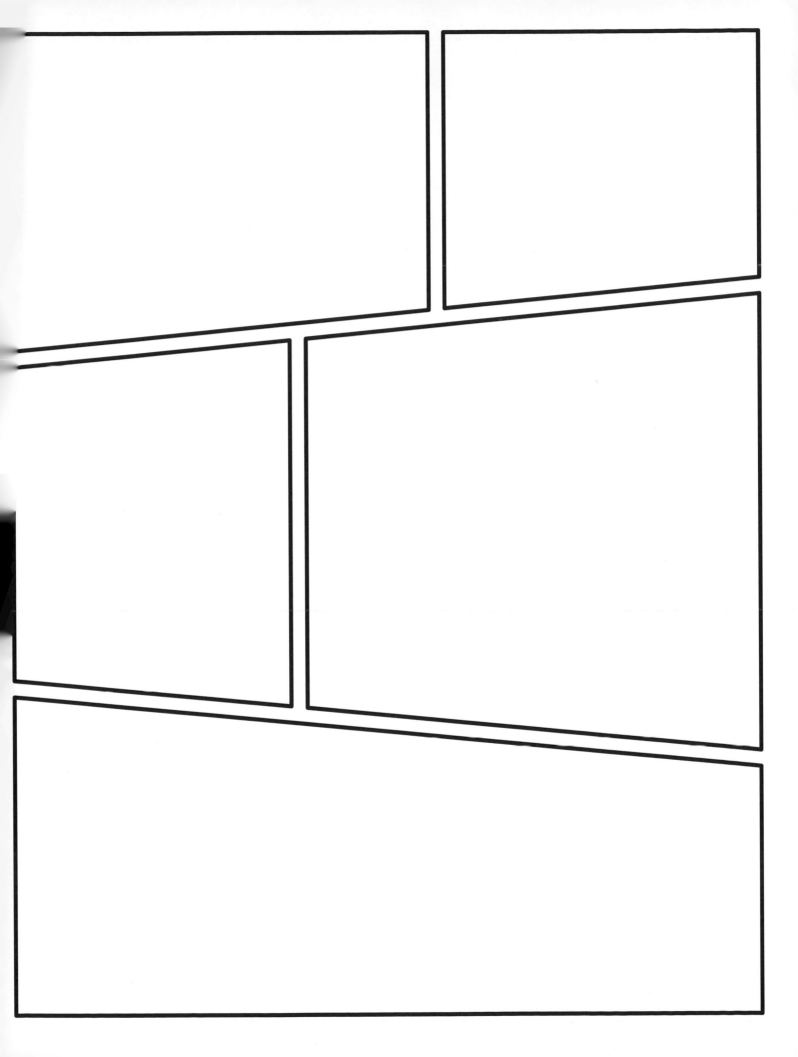

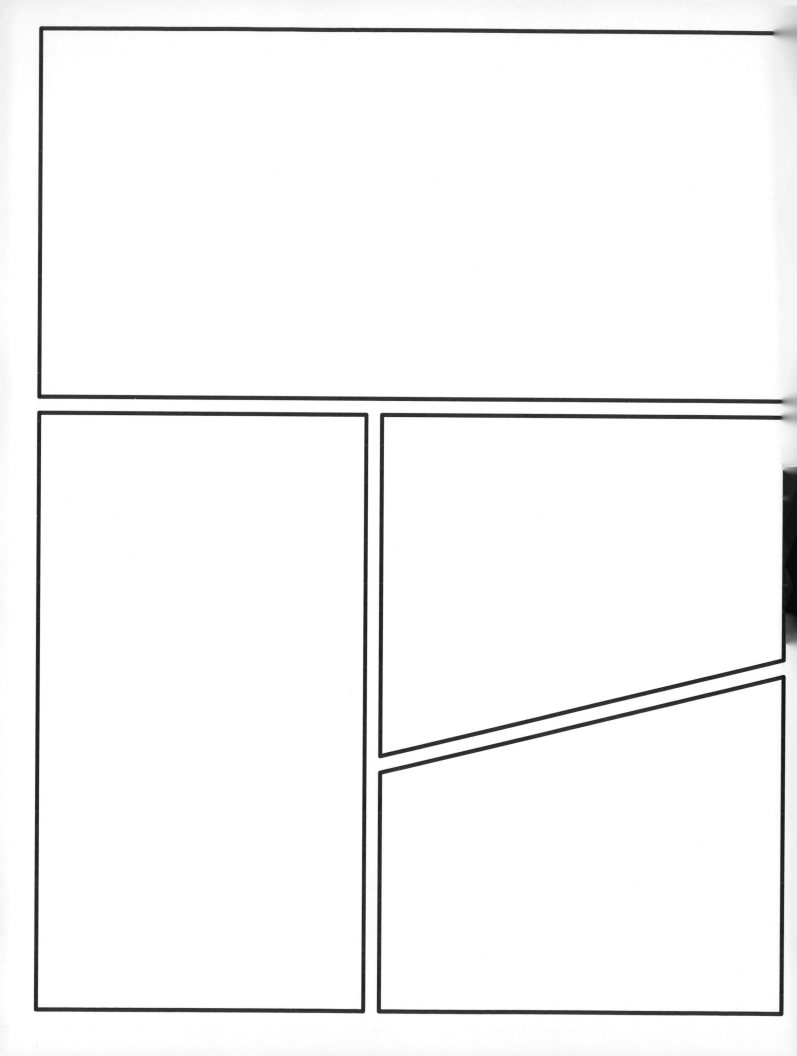

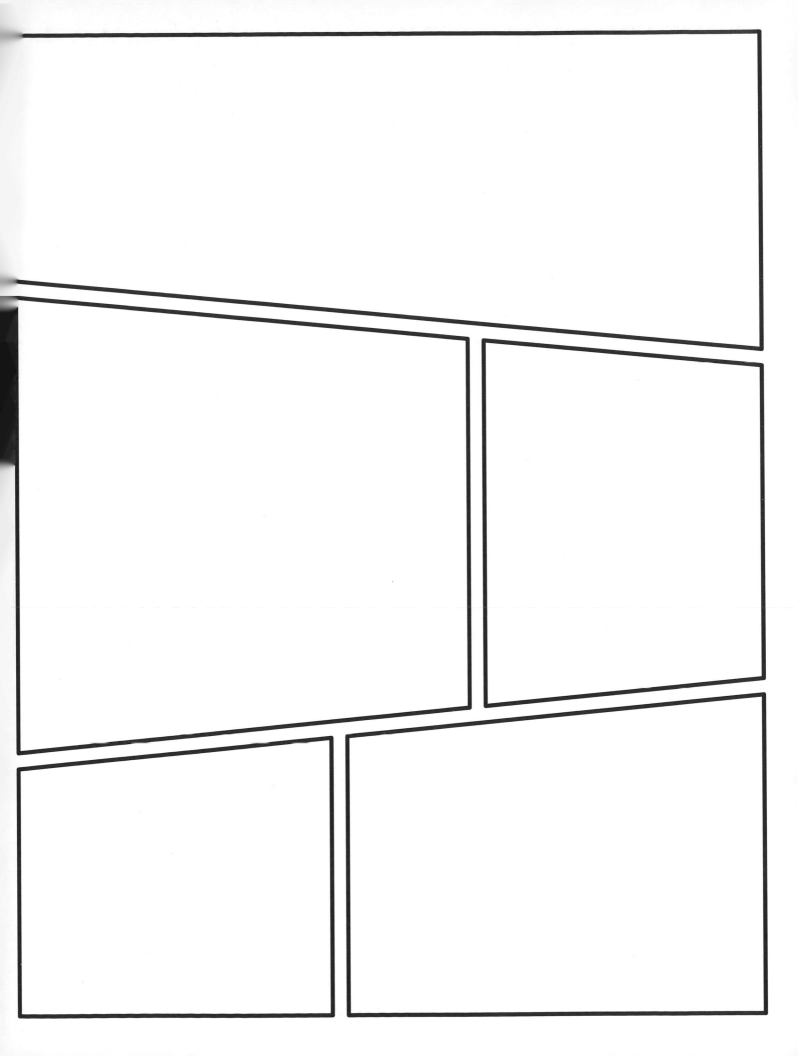

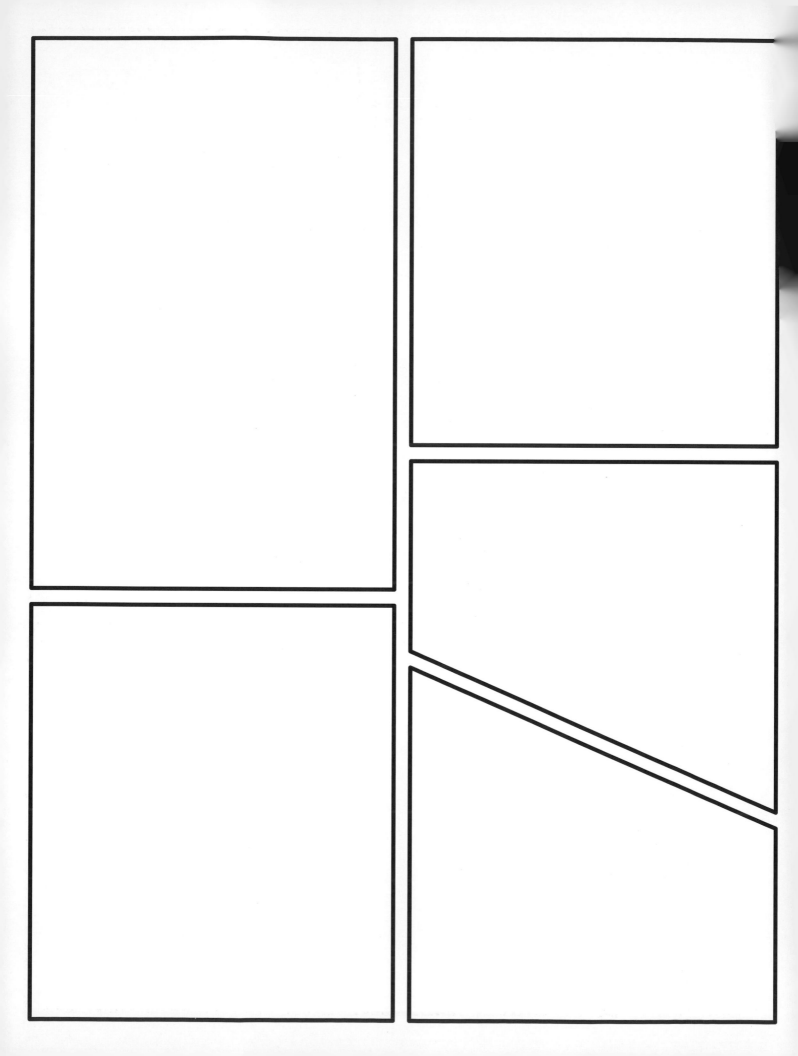

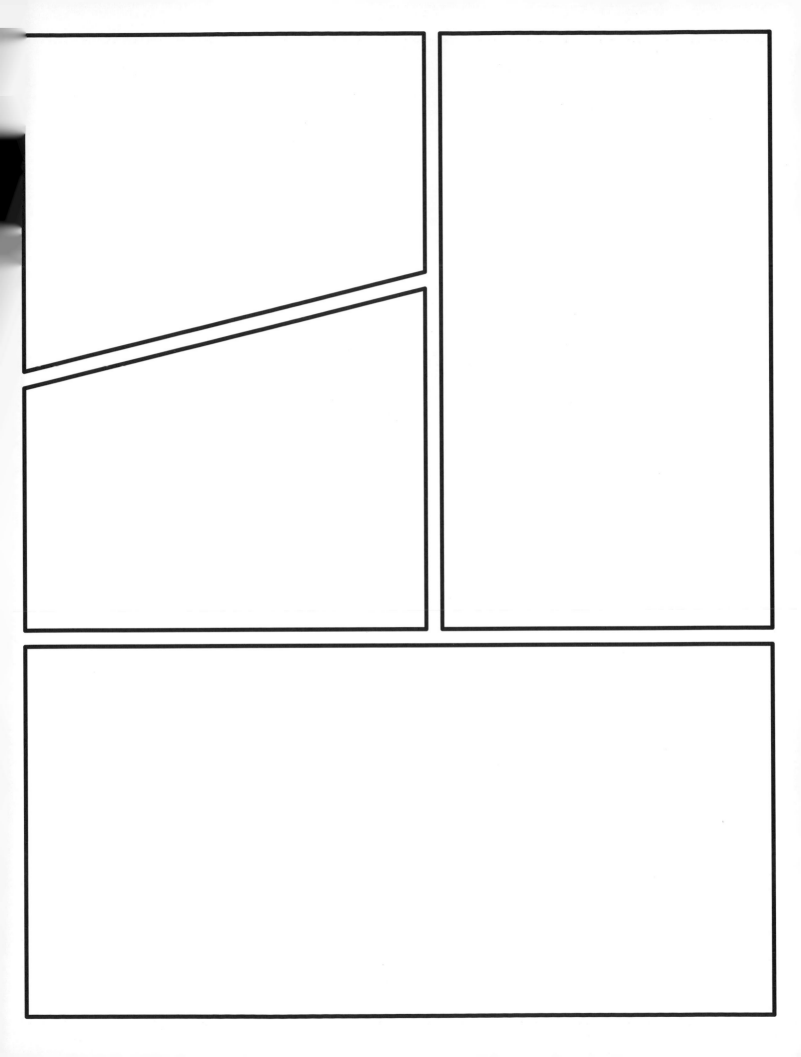

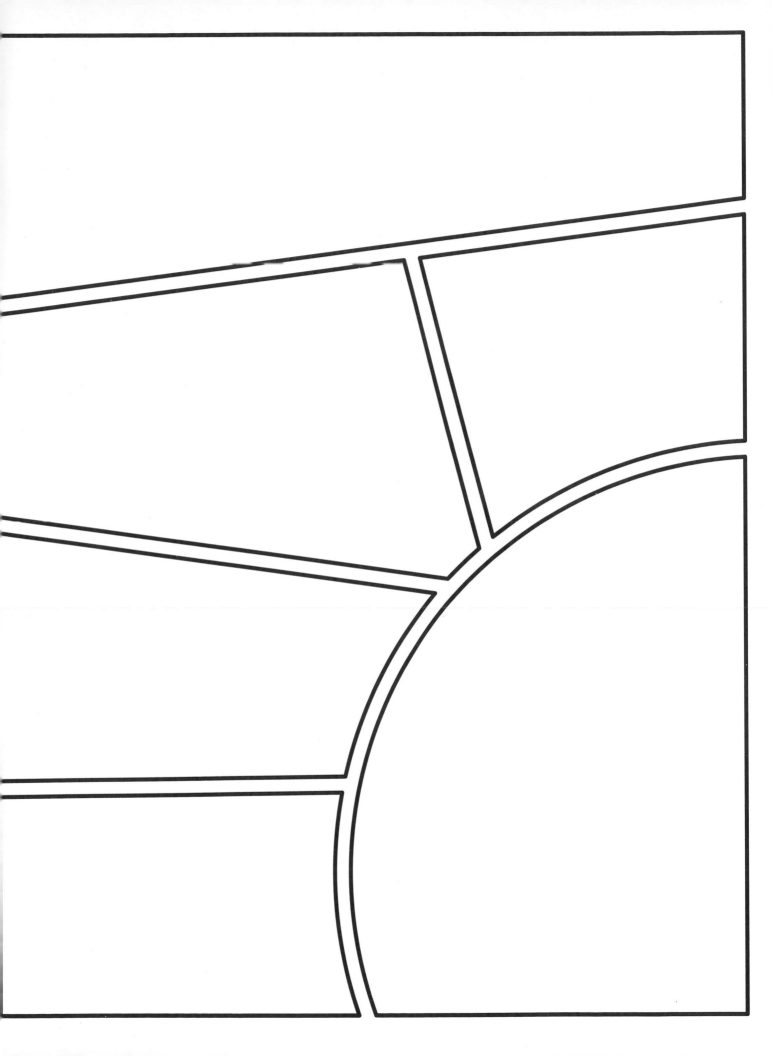

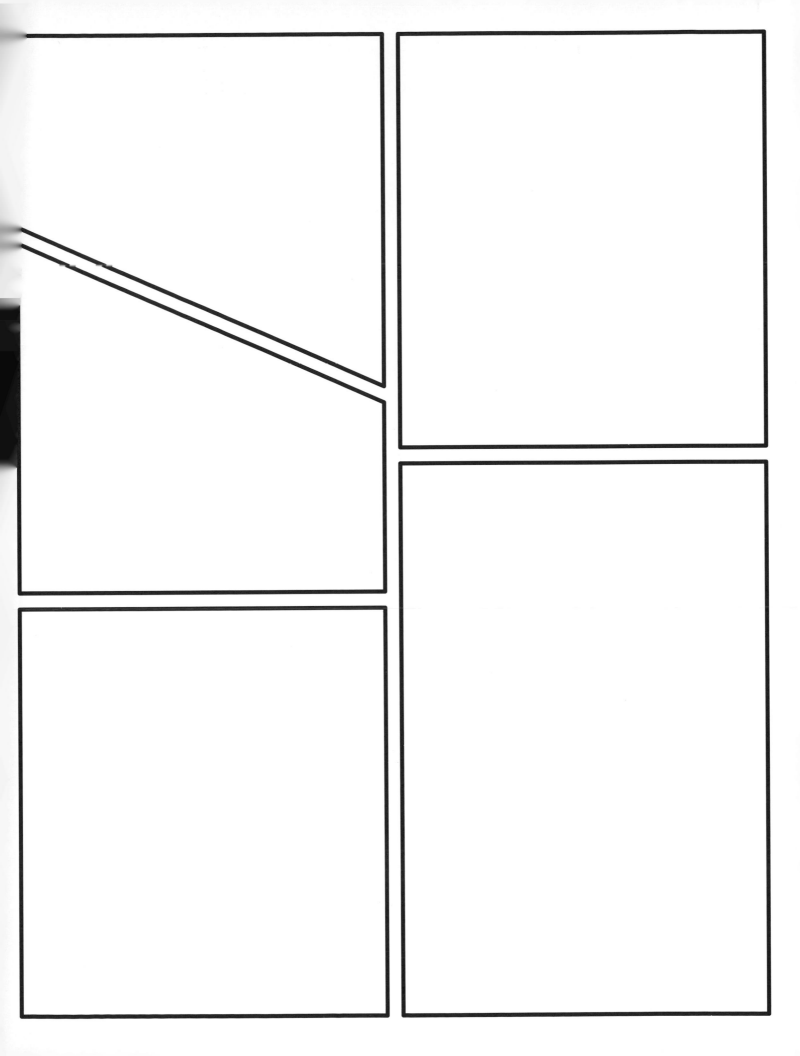

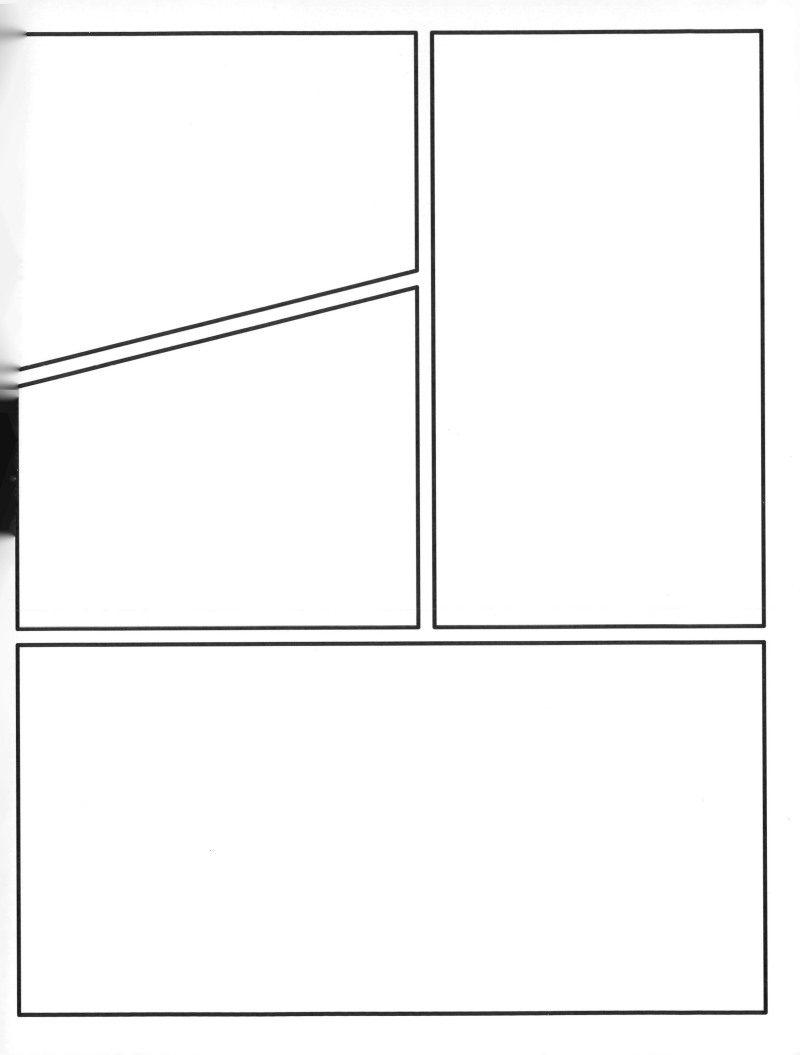

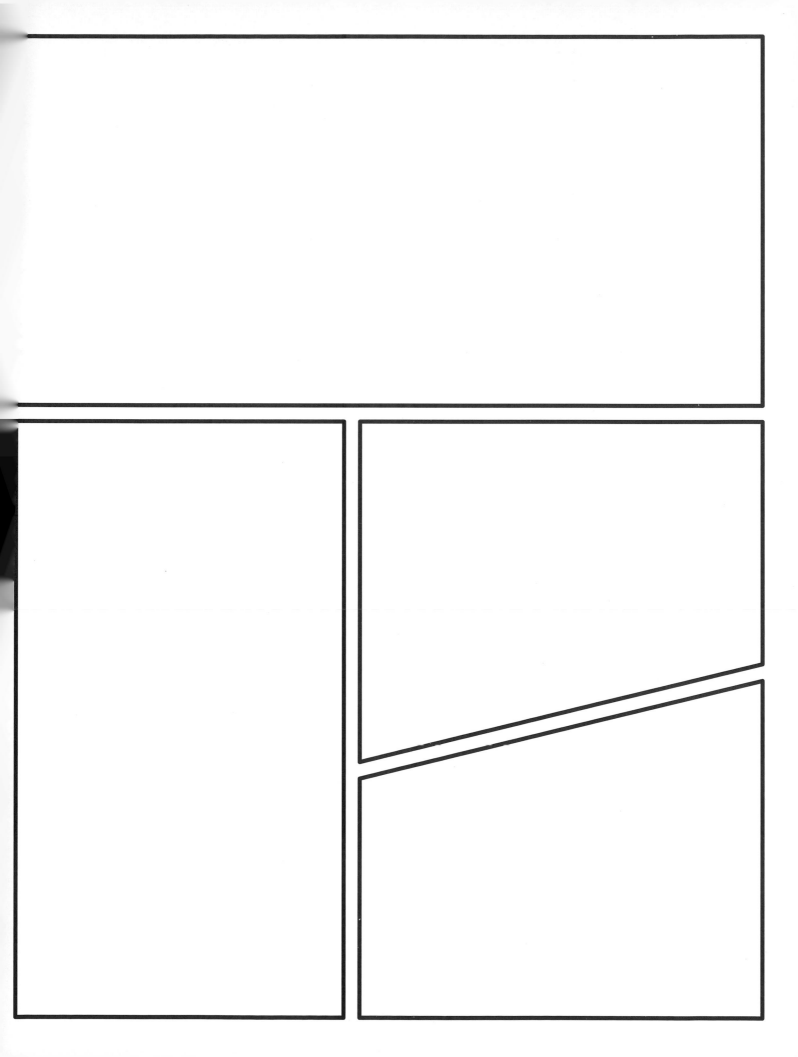

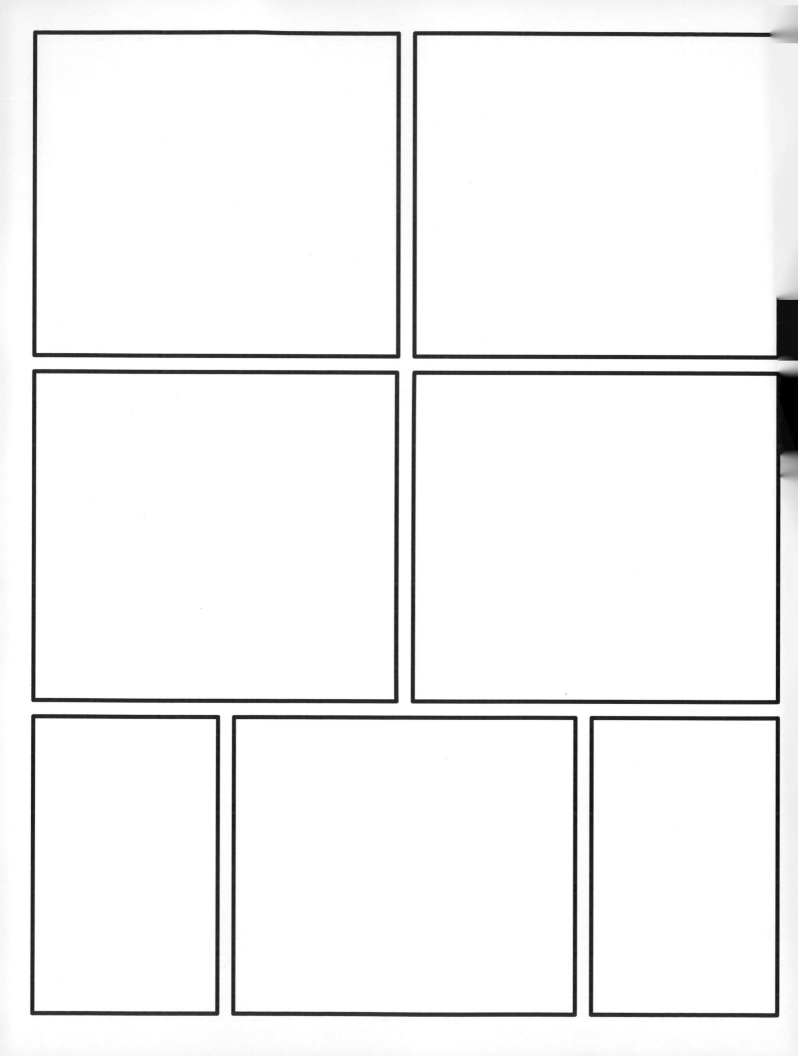

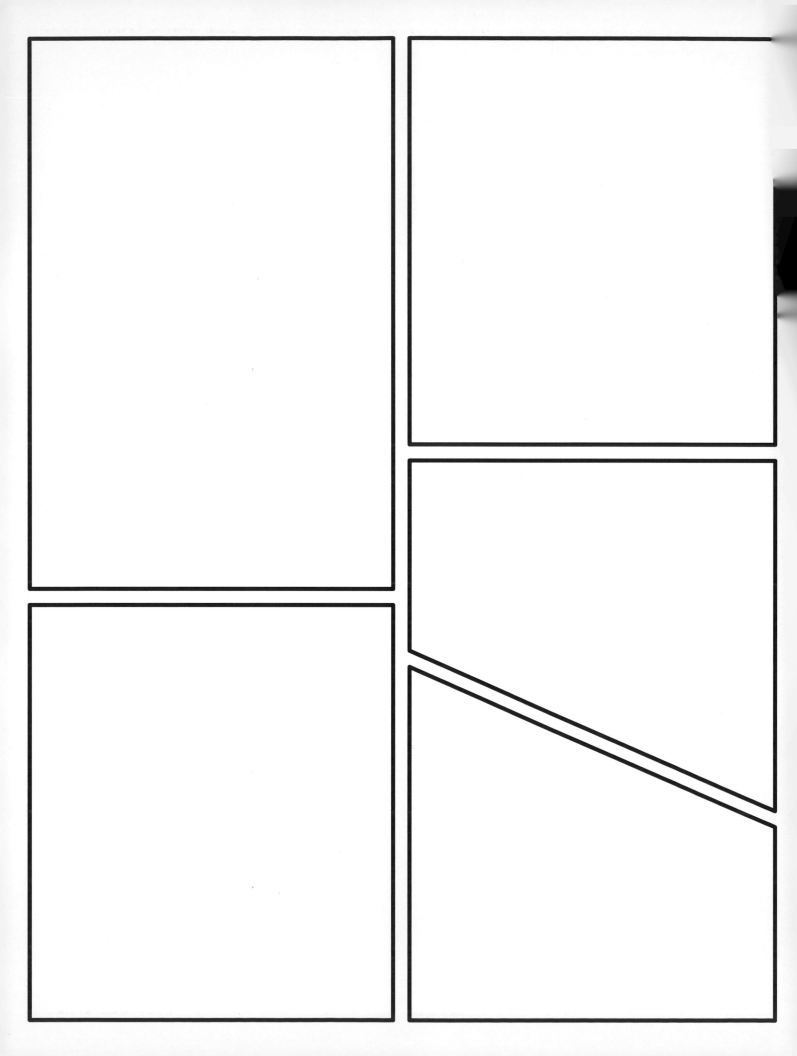

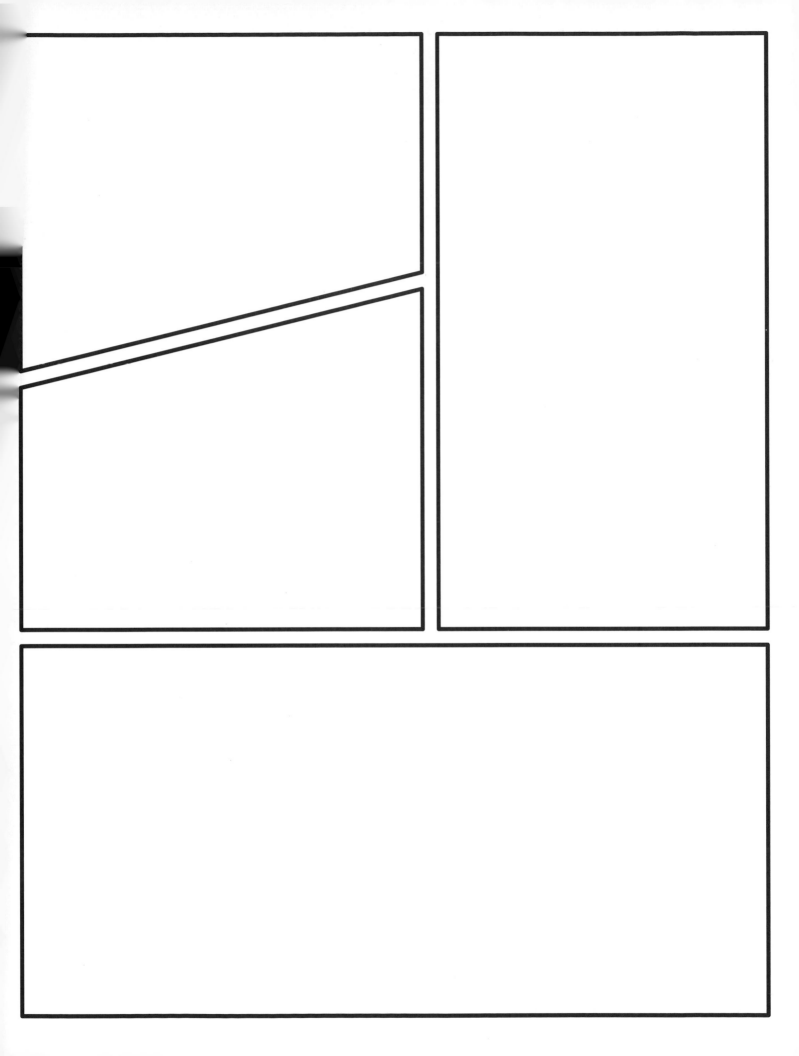

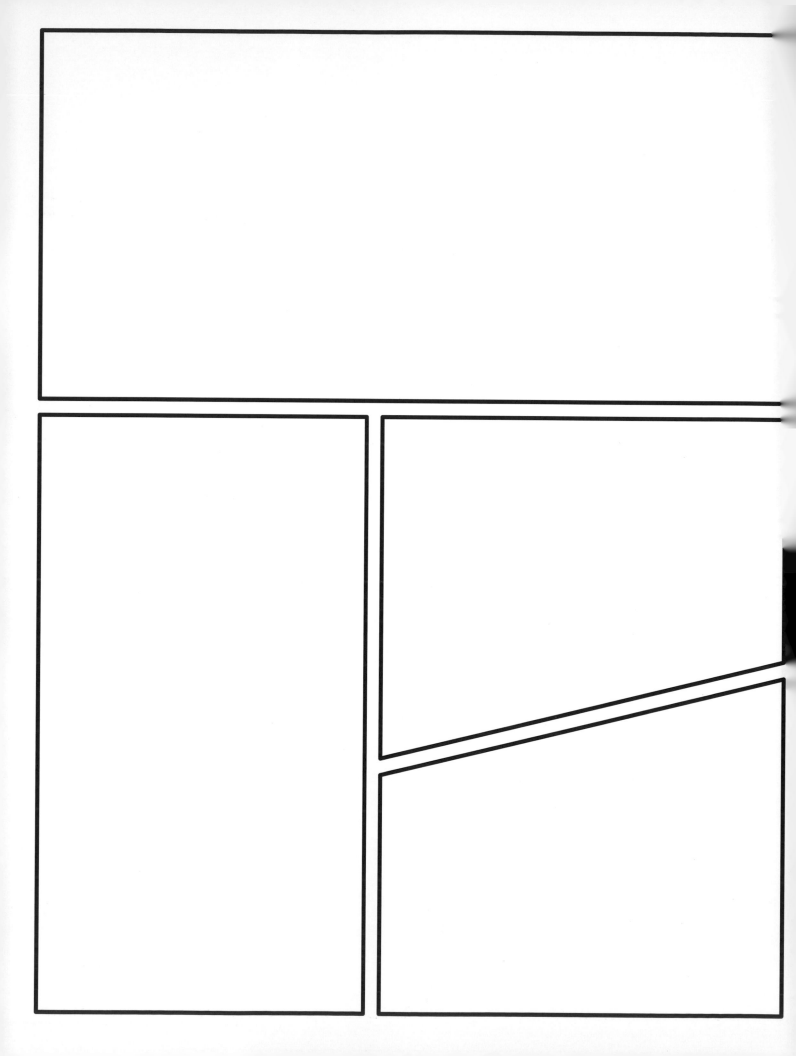

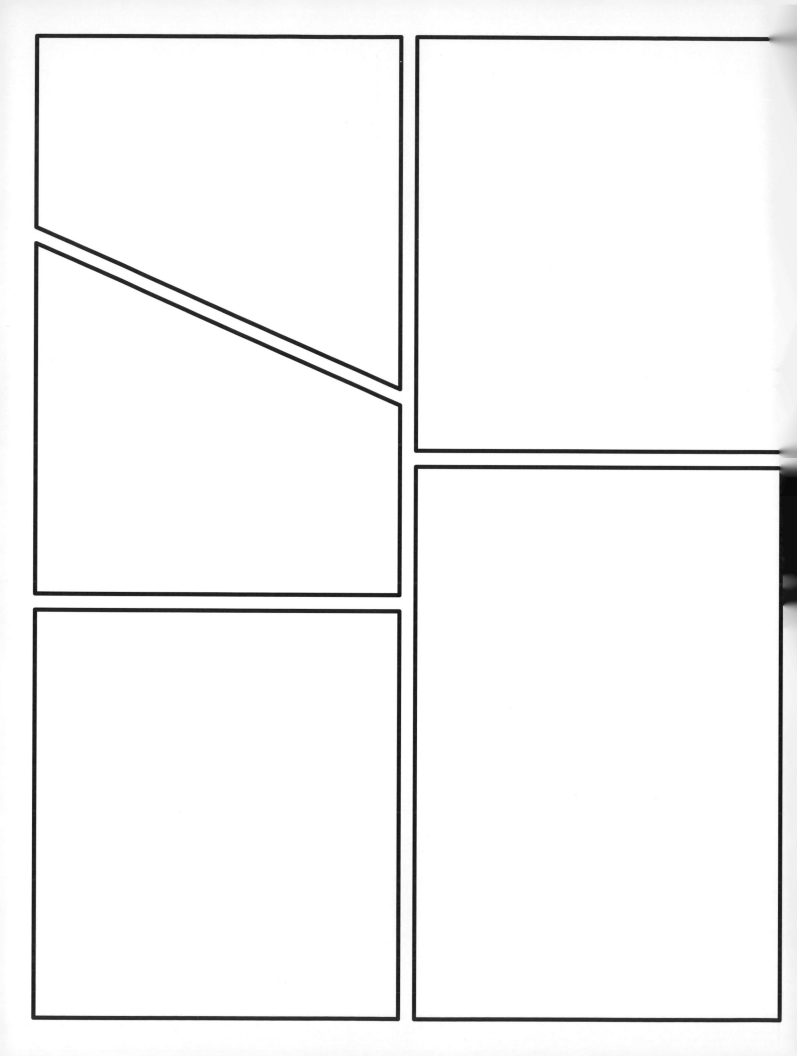

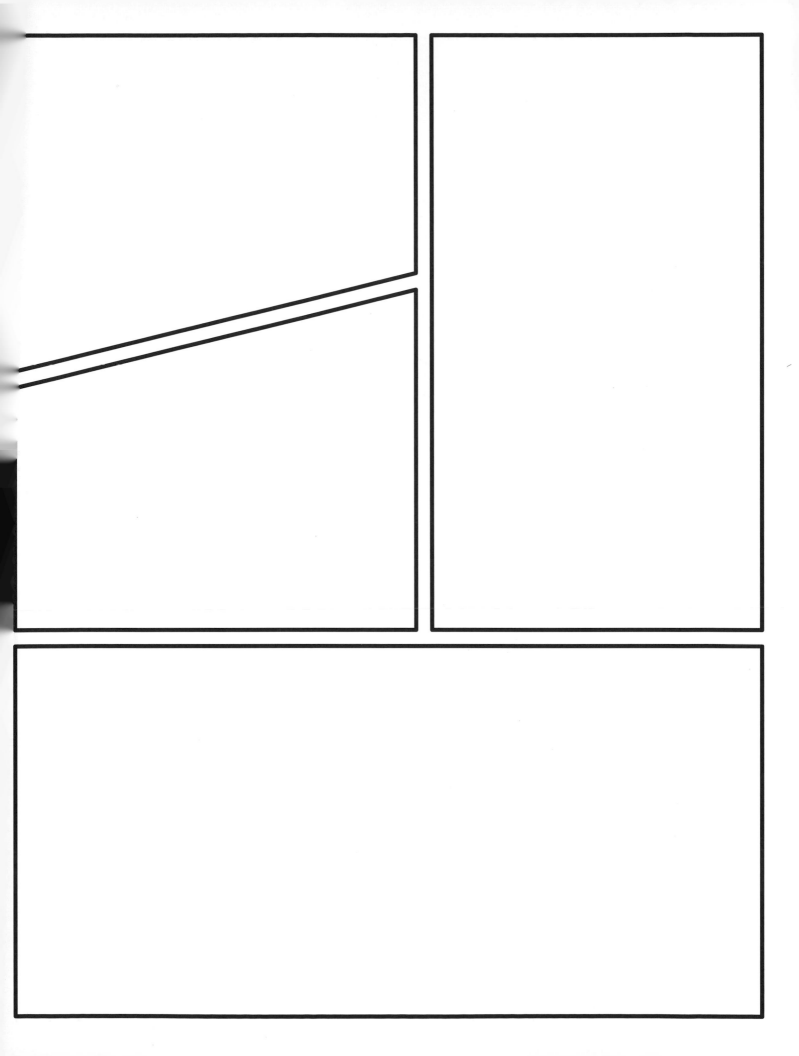

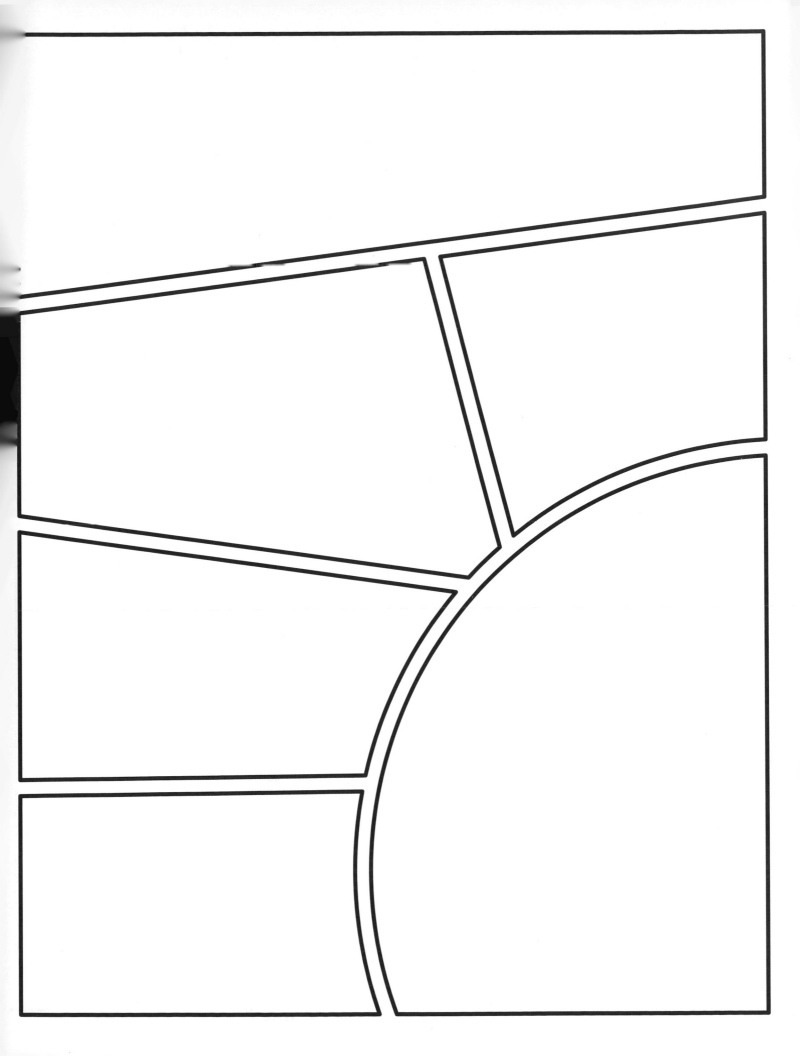

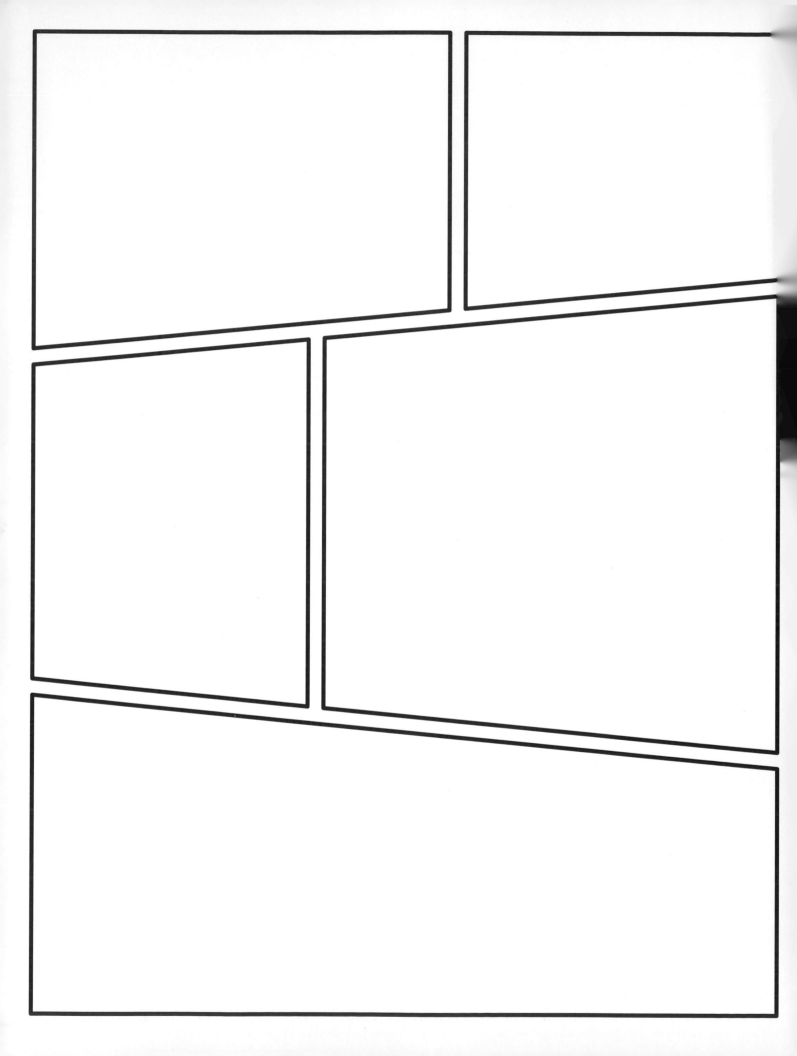

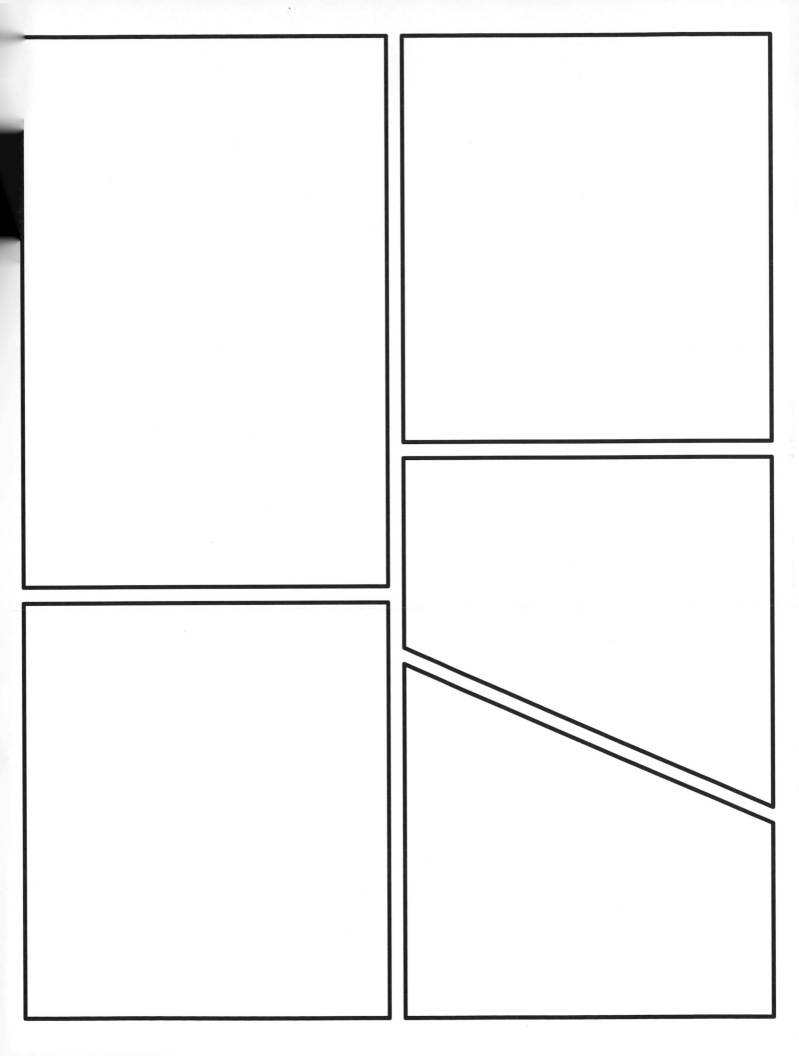

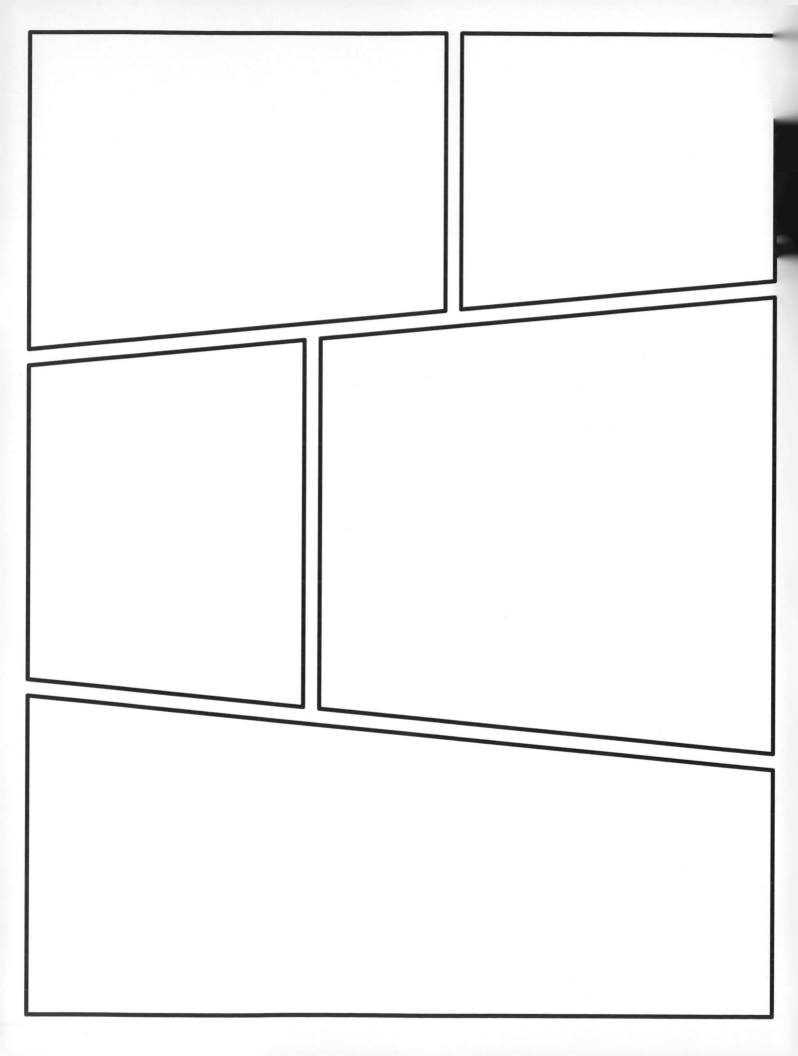

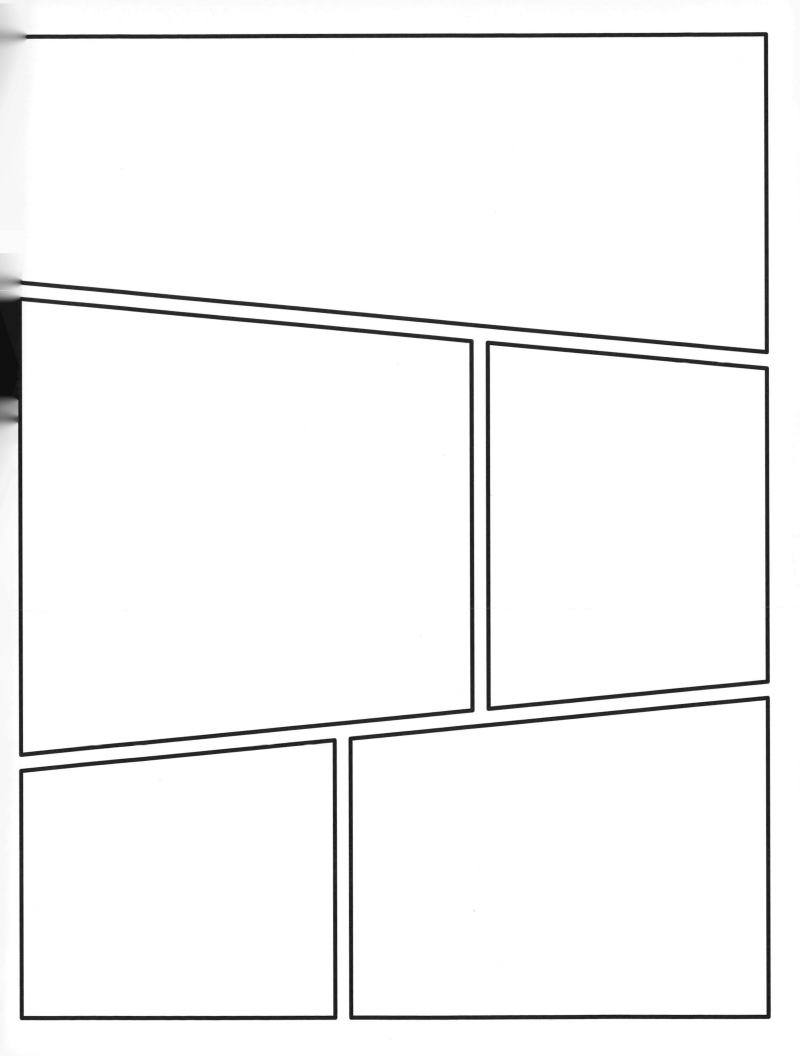

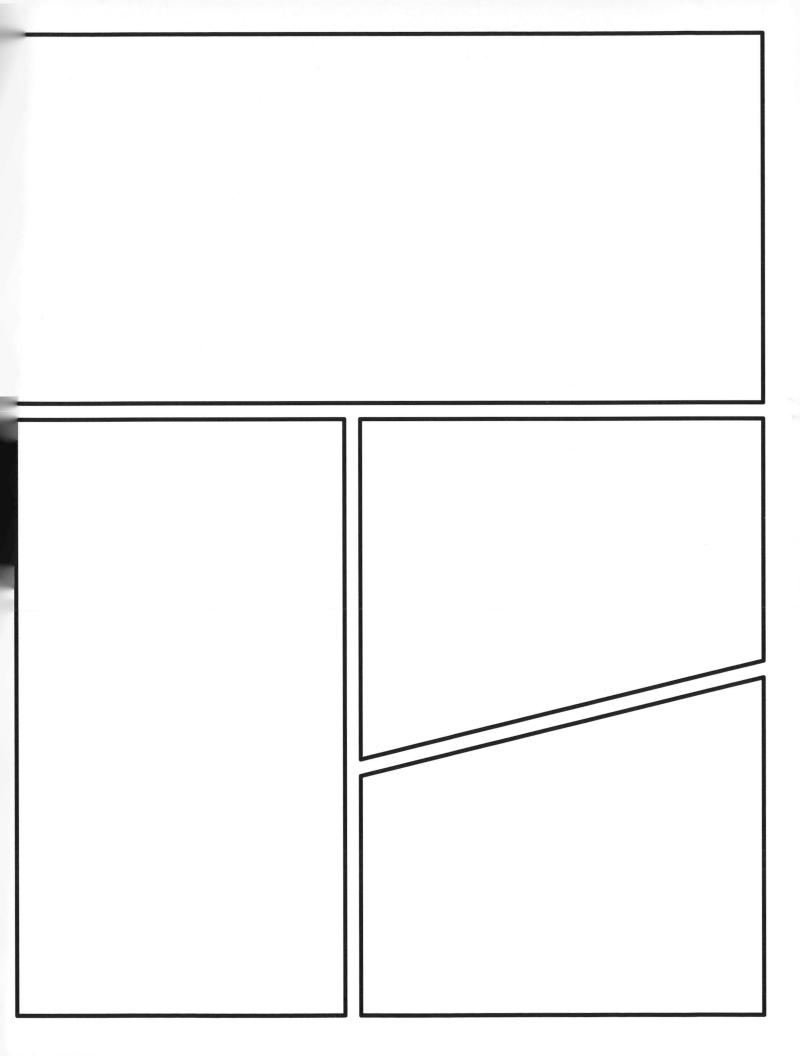

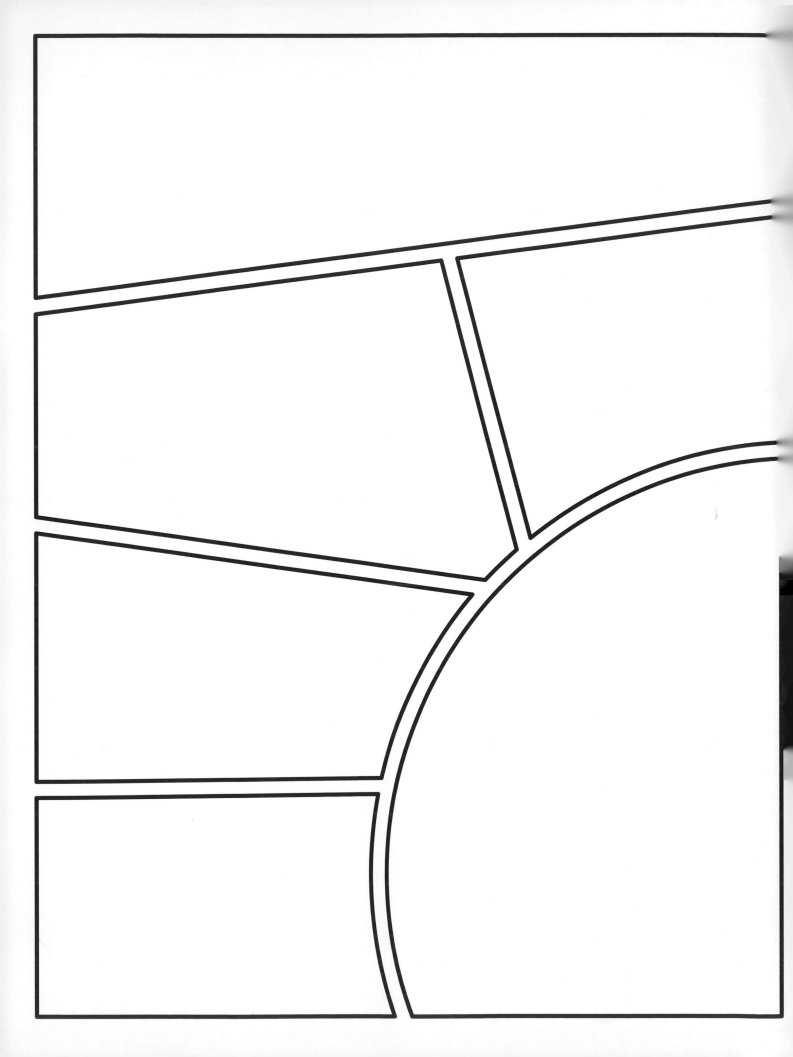

THIS IS A SPEECH BUBBLE.
USE IT WHEN SOMEONE IS TALKING.

THIS IS A THOUGHT BUBBLE.
USE IT WHEN SOMEONE IS THINKING
SOMETHING, BUT NOT SAYING IT OUT LOUD.

A SPIKY SPEECH BUBBLE
MEANS SOMEONE IS SHOUTING.

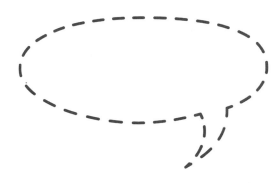

A SPEECH BUBBLE WITH A DASHED OUTLINE
MEANS SOMEONE IS WHISPERING.

A SQUARE SPEECH BUBBLE
CAN MEAN THAT THE WORDS
ARE COMING FROM A TV, RADIO,
OR SPEAKER.

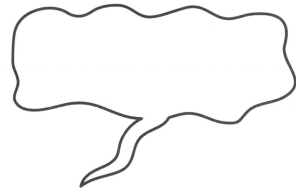

A WAVY SPEECH BUBBLE MAY MEAN THAT
SOMEONE IS DIZZY, CONFUSED, OR GIDDY.

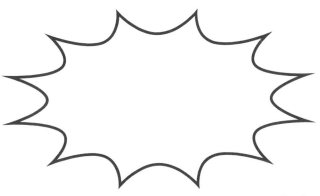

A BURST MAY MEAN THAT SOMETHING IS LOUD,
OR CRASHED INTO SOMETHING ELSE. TRY
USING BURSTS WITH SOUND EFFECTS
LIKE "BAM" AND "POW."

LOTS OF SPEED OR MOTION LINES
MEAN THAT SOMETHING IS MOVING FAST
IN A PARTICULAR DIRECTION.